C0000 008 654 676

D1634238

J
910
9
HUT

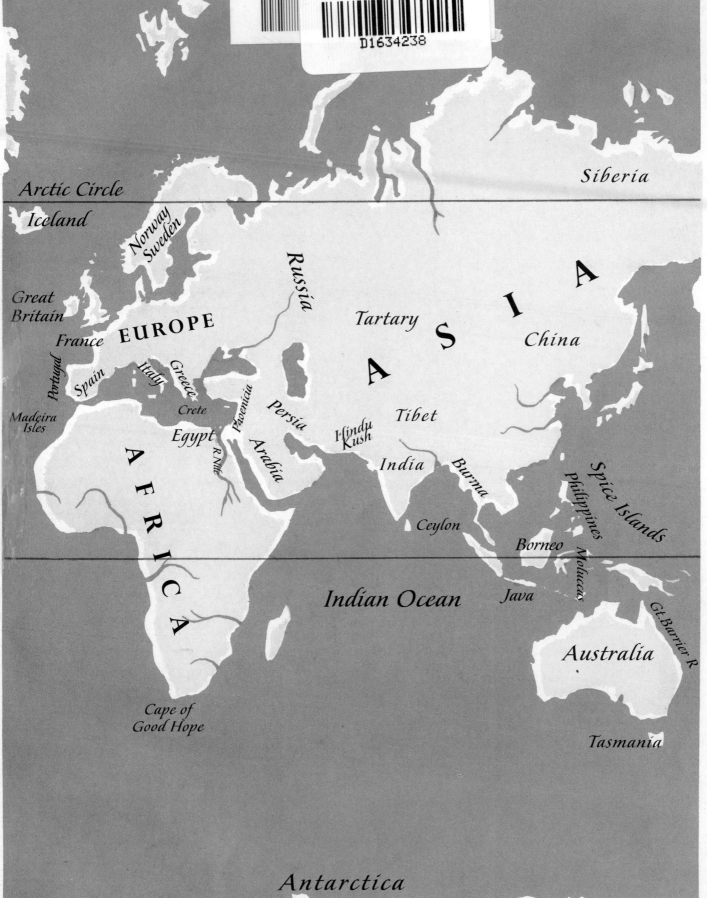

Arctic Circle

Siberia

Iceland

Norway
Sweden

Russia

ASIA

Tartary

China

Great
Britain

France

EUROPE

Portugal

Spain

Italy

Greece

Phoenicia

Persia

Tibet

Crete

Egypt

R.Nile

Arabia

Hindu
Kush

India

Burma

Madeira
Isles

AFRICA

Ceylon

Spice Islands

Philippines

Borneo

Moluccas

Java

Indian Ocean

Gt.Barrier R

Australia

Cape of
Good Hope

Tasmania

Antarctica

# OXFORD
### UNIVERSITY PRESS

Great Clarendon Street, Oxford OX2 6DP

Oxford University Press is a department of the University of Oxford.
It furthers the University's objective of excellence in research, scholarship,
and education by publishing worldwide in

Oxford   New York

Auckland   Cape Town   Dar es Salaam   Hong Kong   Karachi
Kuala Lumpur   Madrid   Melbourne   Mexico City   Nairobi
New Delhi   Shanghai   Taipei   Toronto

With offices in

Argentina   Austria   Brazil   Chile   Czech Republic   France   Greece
Guatemala   Hungary   Italy   Japan   Poland   Portugal   Singapore
South Korea   Switzerland   Thailand   Turkey   Ukraine   Vietnam

Oxford is a registered trade mark of Oxford University Press
in the UK and in certain other countries

Copyright © Oxford University Press 2008

The moral rights of the author have been asserted
Database right Oxford University Press (maker)

First published 1954

This edition 2008

All rights reserved. No part of this publication may be reproduced,
stored in a retrieval system, or transmitted, in any form or by any means,
without the prior permission in writing of Oxford University Press,
or as expressly permitted by law, or under terms agreed with the appropriate
reprographics rights organization. Enquiries concerning reproduction
outside the scope of the above should be sent to the Rights Department,
Oxford University Press, at the address above

You must not circulate this book in any other binding or cover
and you must impose this same condition on any acquirer

British Library Cataloguing in Publication Data

Data available

ISBN: 978-0-19-911835-9

1 3 5 7 9 10 8 6 4 2

Printed in Singapore by Imago

Every care has been taken to trace copyright. In the event of any error, we apologise and will,
if informed, endeavour to make corrections in any future editions.

DRAWN DIRECT TO THE PLATE BY CLARKE HUTTON AND LITHOGRAPHED IN GREAT BRITAIN BY
JESSE BROAD & CO LTD., MANCHESTER

# A
# PICTURE HISTORY
## OF GREAT
# DISCOVERIES

## CLARKE HUTTON
Text written by MABEL GEORGE

**OXFORD**

# Clarke Hutton
## (1898–1984)

Clarke Hutton studied at the Central School of Arts & Crafts in London from 1927–1930 and was taught lithography by A.S. Hartrick, one of the foremost lithographers of his day. On Hartrick's retirement, Clarke Hutton took over his teaching at the School and remained there from 1930–1968.

During this period he became a very well known and respected lithographer. Working largely in this medium he became a successful book illustrator working for a range of publishers including Oxford University Press, Penguin, Dent, The Folio Society and NY Limited Editions Club.

Through his Central School connections he was one of the first artists to use the 'autolithographic technique' for his book illustrations and was part of designer Noel Carrington's team of artists who produced the inexpensive, attractive and innovative Picture Puffins series, along with Pearl Binder, Kathleen Hale and several other Central School artists. He used the same technique for the set of extraordinary, educational prints he produced for Oxford University Press in the 1950s which informatively decorated the walls of many school classrooms of that time.

Like many artists of the period who taught at the Central School, his major contribution can be seen as the passing on of skills and traditions to the next generation, especially illustrators. His students included Peggy Fortnum, Judith Kerr, Susan Einzig, John Burningham and Faith Jaques.

His work forms part of the valuable educational resource of the Central Saint Martins Museum, Archive and Study Collection and is a source of inspiration to new generations of artists, designers and illustrators.

The republishing of this delightful book demonstrates the qualities and role that high quality illustration and visual interpretation still play in stimulating thinking. It might even inspire students to find ways to visually express themselves and the world they live in, through this vibrant and highly personal form of expression, so well presented here by one of Britain's most skilled and inspiring illustrators of the twentieth century.

Chris Wainwright
Dean of Art
Central Saint Martins College of Art and Design

# THE OLD WORLD

In ancient times people believed that the earth was flat with an ocean running round it, and that in those unknown waters lived strange and dangerous monsters. Anyone sailing out over the sea must surely at last sail over the edge of the world, and so for centuries no sailor ventured out of sight of land.

The Egyptians learnt to sail on the Nile, and though sometimes they crossed the sea to Lebanon for cedarwood they were not great seamen. But the Cretans loved the sea. Their many-oared ships could always be seen in the ports of Greece and Italy and Egypt, trading pottery for amber and copper.

The Phoenicians, too, were fearless sailors. Their country was a narrow, barren strip of coast, but it had some good harbours, from which Phoenician ships sailed to all the countries round the Mediterranean, some to trade, others carrying Phoenician families to settle in more fertile lands. These settlers, with their skill in metal work and carving, grew rich and their cities prospered.

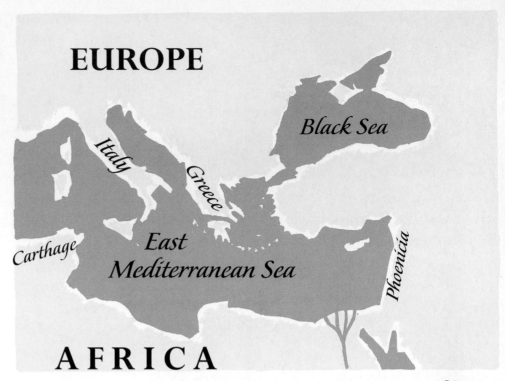

EUROPE

Black Sea

Italy

Greece

Carthage

East
Mediterranean Sea

Phoenicia

AFRICA

But it was not long before Greece began to send her ships over the Mediterranean to try to capture the Phoenician trade. Greeks and Phoenicians became rivals and whenever they met on sea they fought together. Greek scholars, meantime, were learning much from travellers' tales and one day Pythagoras astonished everyone by declaring the world was not flat, but round — like a ball. Another Greek scholar, Hecataeus, wrote two geography books telling all he had learnt about Europe and Asia and including a map showing all the known lands.

While Hecataeus was writing his books, the Phoenicians in Carthage were preparing for a great, secret, colonizing expedition. Admiral Hanno was in charge of a fleet of sixty ships, and thousands of craftsmen, farmers and traders crowded the decks. They passed bravely through the Pillars of Hercules (now called the Straits of Gibraltar) and sailed down the west coast of Africa. On the way they dropped parties of settlers, with food and ships. The rest sailed on into tropical heat and unknown seas. On one island, the local people stoned the intruders so that they fled for their lives. Seeing no prospect of trade in these wild regions Hanno turned back. He had sailed as far as Sierra Leone, and may have reached the Cameroons. It was 2,000 years before white men again sailed so far south along that coast.

Spain

Pillars of Hercules

North West Africa

Sierra Leone

Cameroons

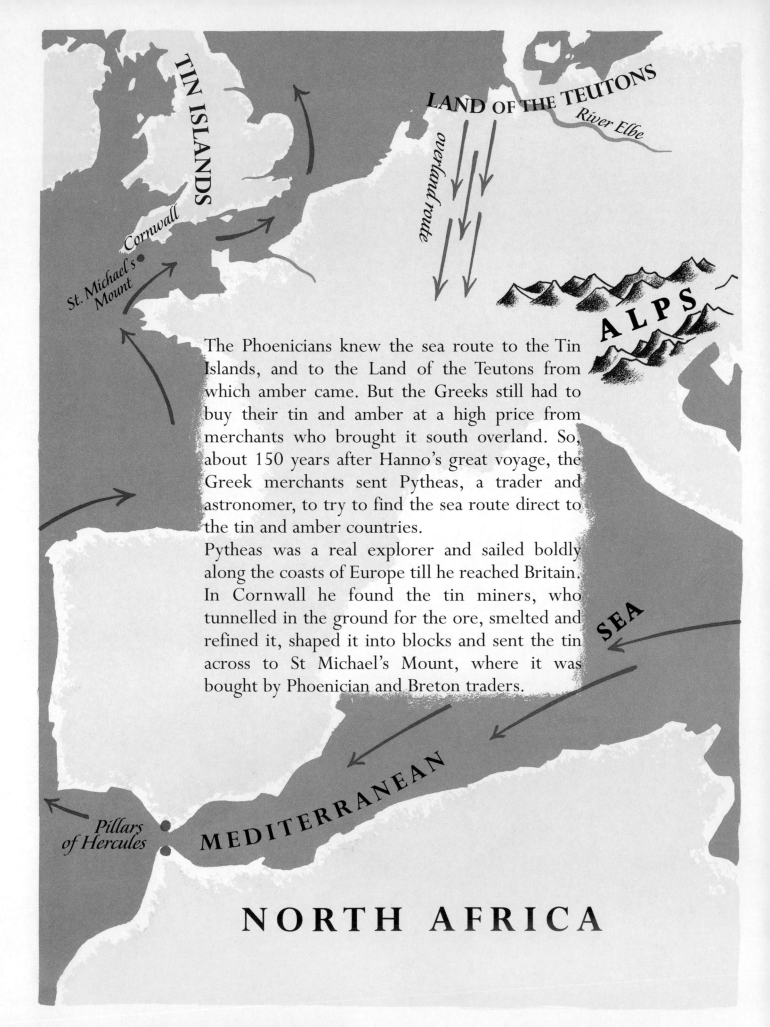

TIN ISLANDS

LAND OF THE TEUTONS

*River Elbe*

*overland route*

ALPS

Cornwall

*St. Michael's Mount*

The Phoenicians knew the sea route to the Tin Islands, and to the Land of the Teutons from which amber came. But the Greeks still had to buy their tin and amber at a high price from merchants who brought it south overland. So, about 150 years after Hanno's great voyage, the Greek merchants sent Pytheas, a trader and astronomer, to try to find the sea route direct to the tin and amber countries.

Pytheas was a real explorer and sailed boldly along the coasts of Europe till he reached Britain. In Cornwall he found the tin miners, who tunnelled in the ground for the ore, smelted and refined it, shaped it into blocks and sent the tin across to St Michael's Mount, where it was bought by Phoenician and Breton traders.

SEA

*Pillars of Hercules*

MEDITERRANEAN

NORTH AFRICA

Pytheas sailed all round Britain, exploring the country, observing the people, their houses and habits. After some time he crossed the Channel and sailed north along the European coast. Near the mouth of the River Elbe the Teutons told him that amber was to be found on the small island of Heligoland; and when he landed there Pytheas saw men and women gathering the raw amber in baskets on the seashore.

While Pytheas was exploring in the north, a new king had arisen in Macedonia at the head of a powerful army. His name was Alexander and his heart was set on conquest. Already master of Greece, in 330 B.C. he marched on Persia who was unprepared for attack and easily overthrown. King Darius was killed and the remnant of the Persian army fled into Bactria, pursued by Alexander.

Across Bactria and into the hard, mountainous country of Afghanistan Alexander led his men, fighting, conquering. In the Hindu Kush mountains he was forced to halt for the winter, but in the spring he marched on again, capturing and killing the Persian leader, but never checking his victorious progress. He crossed Turkestan and was almost at the gates of China when he decided to turn back into India where he knew great riches lay.

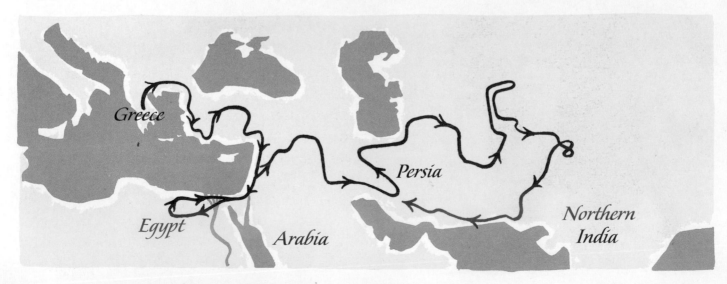

Greece

Egypt

Arabia

Persia

Northern India

His fame ran before him and many Indian princes yielded in fear; those who did not were ruthlessly destroyed. It seemed all the world must fall before him, but at the River

Beas Alexander's faithful horse died under him; and his army mutinied.

Officers and men, battle-weary, refused to go further, and after erecting a bronze column bearing the inscription 'Here Alexander Halted' the conqueror set his face for home.

Persia

Afghanistan

North
India

Arabia

But first he appointed Nearchus admiral of a small fleet and ordered him to open up a sea route between India and Persia. Some of the army embarked in the ships, the rest Alexander led overland on a terrible trek through southern Persia, during which hundreds of soldiers died. Alexander's conquests added many new lands to the map; and for over 300 years sailors used the long sea route that Nearchus had opened to the East.

When Greece came under the power of Rome, the spices and silks, jewels and perfumes Greek sailors brought from the East helped the Romans to become the most rich and cultured people in the western world.

Then Hippalus, a young sailor living early in the first century, opened a new era in the history of the sea. He was the first sailor brave enough to sail before the monsoon wind straight across the Indian Ocean. The monsoon was called Hippalus wind, after him.

Other sailors soon followed in his wake, and one Roman trader even sailed on the monsoon across the Sea of Bengal to Burma and Malaya, and on to Cochin-China, where he saw Chinese people for the first time.

The old maps were useless. Everyone knew now that spices did not come from Paradise (which the old mapmakers had always drawn in their maps) but from India and the islands of the east.

In 150 A.D. Ptolemy drew a new map. It showed all the known lands, and though he made Asia too large and left very little room for unknown regions, Ptolemy's was the best map ever made till that time and was used for hundreds of years.

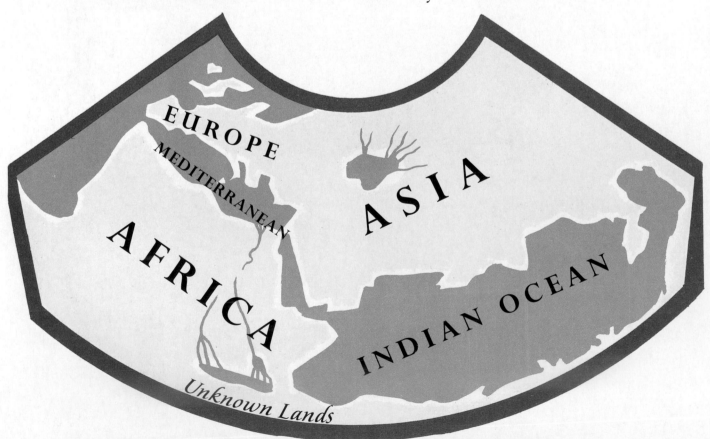

But the Roman Empire was tottering and the Arabs were forcing Greeks and Romans off their seas. The East was closed to them and their civilization was overrun by barbarians from the north. For 800 years Europe lay in the grip of the Dark Ages.

In the north Vikings were voyaging to Iceland and Greenland and even to North America, but their achievements were not known outside their own country and their discoveries were not added to the map.

# THE TRAVELS OF MARCO POLO

In 1010 Christian knights all over Europe began to rise against the Arabs who crushed the Holy Land under a heathen heel. The Crusades lasted for over 200 years and though no decisive victory came for Christian or Infidel, knowledge of the East was brought once more to Europe.

Asia, too, was again opened early in the thirteenth century. The Tartars had conquered all lands from China to the Black Sea and European traders were free to enter the East by the roads the Grand Khan's armies had made.

Marco Polo, an intelligent Venetian lad of seventeen, travelled on these roads with his father and uncle to the Court of the Grand Khan Kublai in Peking. He used his eyes, and made notes of all he saw: the strong Persian ox, the Bactrian sheep that stored food in its great tail as a camel does in its hump; the strong-walled Persian cities.

In Peking Marco Polo found favour with the Grand Khan who made him one of his officers. He even wore their long silk robe, and was sent on the Khan's business to the farthest corners of his wide realm.

The Chinese he found polite and wise. Noblemen always wore their fingernails very long, and the most beautiful ladies were those with the tiniest feet. Marco Polo saw coal for the first time, and paper money and books printed. There was a postal service operating on well-made roads, the 'postmen' being fast runners who ran in relays, with packets and letters. In the cities there were baths where 100 people might bathe at once.

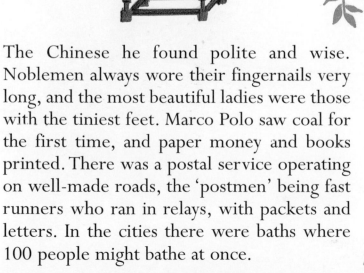

Marco Polo wrote of the wonderful painted palaces of the Khan, and of how Kublai rode forth to hunt reclining in a little house erected on the backs of four elephants, while thousands of attendants ran below and peasants burnt spices outside their doors to perfume the royal way.

He told of crocodiles, of the dog sleds and white bears of Siberia, the tigers of Tibet; of the shining towers of Burma with bells that rang sweetly in the wind; of Java and Japan where precious spices grew.

When he returned to Venice by sea in 1295, Marco Polo wrote a book on his travels, and mapmakers drew another map showing all the new lands and the routes Marco Polo had opened by land and sea.

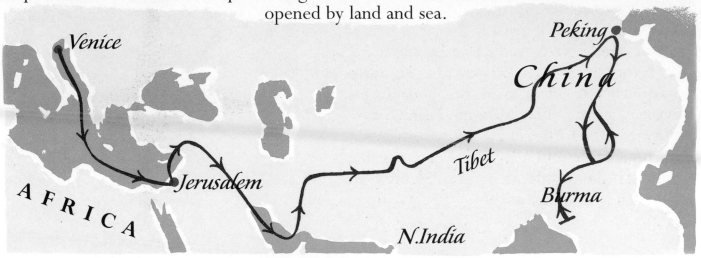

# HENRY THE NAVIGATOR

When the Tartar Empire collapsed and Turks and Arabs again blocked the way to the East, Prince Henry of Portugal determined to find a way to India round the south of Africa.

He shut himself up in a tower with mapmakers, navigators and shipbuilders, and all the books on geography he could find. He became known as Henry the Navigator.

The ships he built were the best in Europe and were called caravels. His sailors carried compass and astrolabe so that they could sail far out to sea without getting lost.

But his captains were cautious and it was many years before the fine caravels sailed as far down the African coast as Hanno had gone in his heavy rowboats. The Madeira Islands were discovered, and African people were brought to Portugal to be sold as servants, thus starting the African slave trade. But when Henry died in 1460 his ships had not yet reached the tip of Africa.

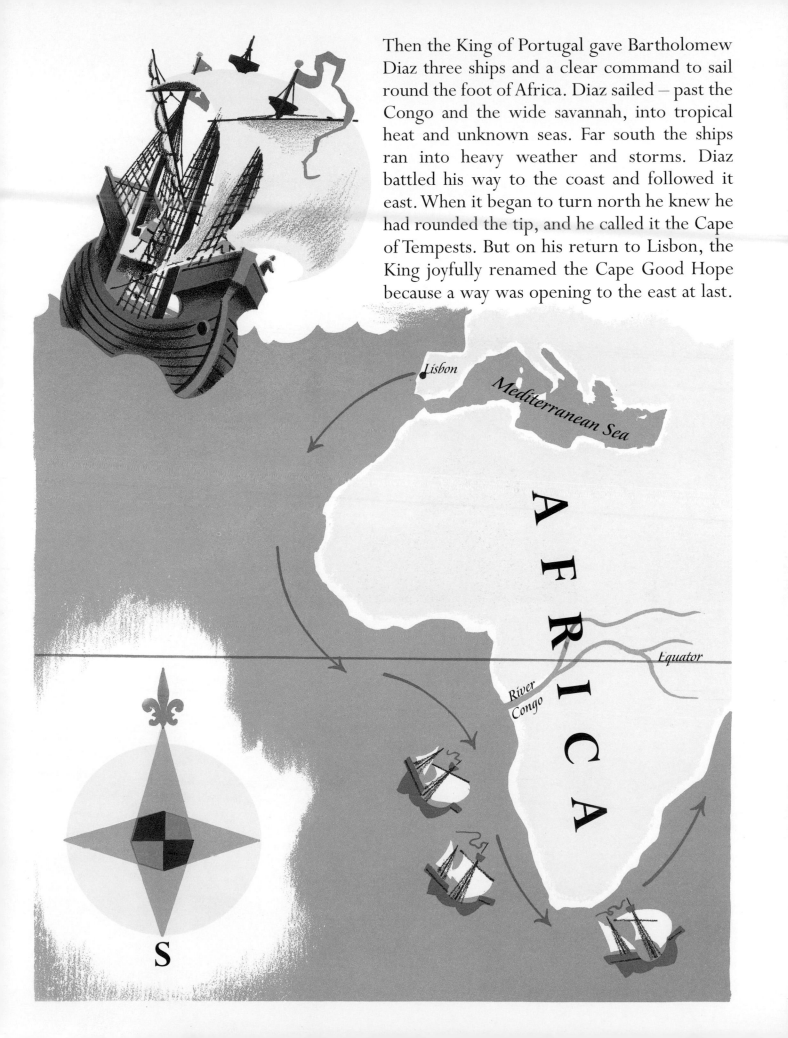

Then the King of Portugal gave Bartholomew Diaz three ships and a clear command to sail round the foot of Africa. Diaz sailed – past the Congo and the wide savannah, into tropical heat and unknown seas. Far south the ships ran into heavy weather and storms. Diaz battled his way to the coast and followed it east. When it began to turn north he knew he had rounded the tip, and he called it the Cape of Tempests. But on his return to Lisbon, the King joyfully renamed the Cape Good Hope because a way was opening to the east at last.

Lisbon

Mediterranean Sea

AFRICA

Equator

River Congo

S

# THE NEW WORLD

Christopher Columbus was an Italian, born at Genoa in 1451. He came to Lisbon while the Portuguese were still looking for the tip of Africa, and helped his brother paint maps and sometimes sailed in caravels. It seemed to him, as he studied Ptolemy's map, that if a ship sailed into the west from Portugal she must at last come to the Spice Islands and Japan. The King of Portugal would not listen to his wild idea, but the King of Spain agreed to give him three ships and a rich reward if his venture was successful.

So with his little ships, the *Santa Maria*, *Pinta* and *Nina*, Columbus sailed out of the Port of Palos in August, 1492, and steered into the setting sun. In October he saw land ahead, and the ships brought up off an island in the Bahamas.

Astonished men ran and shouted on the sandy shore, and Columbus was perplexed. He was expecting to see the rich lands and cultivated people of China or Japan. But he landed in state and gave the

local people presents of beads, bells and knives. They in turn presented him with fruits and cotton balls, green parrots and arrows. Columbus captured seven of the men to present to the King of Spain and sailed on to Cuba.

He supposed this must be China, but here the local people had the curious habit of smoking large leaves, dried and rolled. It was tobacco.

Columbus went on to Haiti, which was a garden of fruits and birds.

When he returned, Spain welcomed him with fanfares and flying banners and his fame spread throughout Europe.

The Pope, fearing these new discoveries might cause quarrels between Spain and Portugal, took a map and drew a line down the centre. To Spain he gave the western half, and to Portugal the east.

Soon Columbus was off again, carrying many people who wished to settle in the new lands. In Haiti the first Spanish city in America – Isabella – was built.

Twice more Columbus crossed the Atlantic discovering new lands on each voyage, but never finding his way through to the Spice Islands and Asia, so that he died disappointed soon after his fourth voyage without knowing he had added one of the greatest and richest continents to the map of the world.

Adventurous Spaniards were quick to follow where Columbus had led. In 1497 Amerigo Vespucci discovered the coast of Mexico and the east coast of what is now the U.S.A. and gave his name – America – to the continent. Balboa, a soldier of fortune, crossed the Isthmus of Panama and from a hilltop saw spread below him the vast Pacific Ocean.

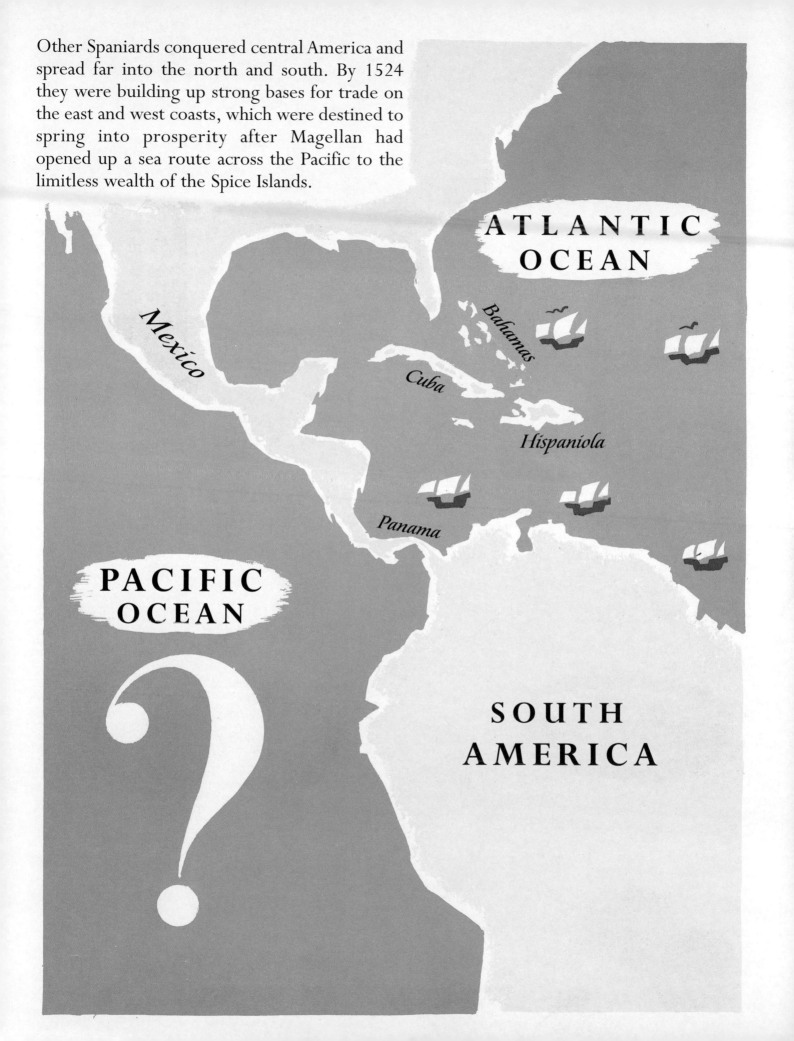

Other Spaniards conquered central America and spread far into the north and south. By 1524 they were building up strong bases for trade on the east and west coasts, which were destined to spring into prosperity after Magellan had opened up a sea route across the Pacific to the limitless wealth of the Spice Islands.

ATLANTIC
OCEAN

*Mexico*

*Bahamas*

*Cuba*

*Hispaniola*

*Panama*

PACIFIC
OCEAN

SOUTH
AMERICA

# VASCO DA GAMA

The Portuguese were still persisting in their efforts to reach India round the foot of Africa. Vasco da Gama was appointed admiral of a fleet of four ships, two being specially built by Bartholomew Diaz to resist the hard weather of the Cape. They were splendidly fitted out, well armed and supplied with the finest instruments. The fleet sailed slowly down the African coast, where already the Portuguese were trading peacefully with the natives in gold and ivory, wax, skins and sugar. Near the Cape they put ashore for fresh water, and a local man was captured and brought before the admiral, who gave him presents and let him go.

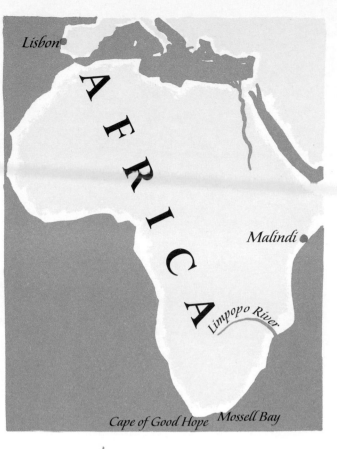

After rounding the stormy Cape the ships lay off Mossell Bay, and the sailors drove some hard bargains with the simple natives: a fine ox being exchanged for three cheap bracelets.

It was Christmas time as they sailed on up the east coast and da Gama called the country they were passing Natal in honour of the birth of Christ. Anchor was dropped near the Limpopo River in the country of the Bantu natives – tall, brave hunters, generous and friendly.

Further north da Gama ran against hostile Arab ships, whose captains were angry and surprised to find Portuguese sails over their waters. But da Gama's guns quelled his enemies, and he was kindly received in Malindi, an Arab town ruled by a Persian king whose gifts of fresh meat and fruit were very welcome to the scurvy-ridden sailors.

Guided by an Indian pilot the ships crossed the Indian Ocean to Calicut, da Gama being the first European to land in India since Roman times. By permission of the Zamorin (ruler) he traded freely in Calicut, which was a collecting port for all the merchandise of the East. His holds were filled with spices, jewels, silks and furs, ivory, gold and silver.

When the monsoon brought more angry Arabs da Gama sailed for home. So many of the crews died from scurvy he had only enough men left to man one ship. The remaining ships were broken up, and the *San Gabriel* alone completed the arduous voyage round Africa to drop anchor in Lisbon harbour.

# FERDINAND MAGELLAN

When Vasco da Gama returned to Lisbon in 1498 Ferdinand Magellan was a lad of eighteen who longed to go to sea. He joined the King's ships and served in the East Indies, rising to Captain's rank and owning a Sumatran slave. But Magellan's greatest ambition was to find the passage that the Spaniards were still seeking through America to the Spice Islands.

The captain's blunt manners and air of arrogance had never pleased the Portuguese king, so Magellan took his plans to the King of Spain. He was given five ships – the *Trinidad*, *San Antonio*, *Victoria*, *Conception* and *Santiago* – and a young Italian, Pigafetta, who was to keep a diary of the voyage.

In September 1519 Magellan set sail, crossing to the Bay of Brazil and sailing down the American coast. Beyond the River Plate the weather became wintry and seals and penguins were seen on shore. Magellan decided to anchor for the winter in a large bay. After two months without a sight of any other human beings, the crews saw a tall, naked man on the shore. He danced and sprinkled sand on his head, obviously wishing to be friendly. He brought more of his tribe, and because of their large feet the sailors called them Patagones (*patagoas* meaning 'big feet' in Spanish), and their country is still called Patagonia.

*Patagonia S.America*

*Brazil*

In the spring Magellan continued south, watching closely for an opening. It appeared at last: a narrow channel overhung with hills. The ships sailed slowly through. Certain men were sent forward in a rowboat to investigate, and returned shouting that the open sea lay ahead. Magellan wept for joy and called the passage the Channel of the Saints (it has since been renamed Magellan Strait in his honour).

The *Santiago* had been wrecked on the Patagonian coast, and the Spanish officers of the *San Antonio*, who had long resented Magellan because he was Portuguese, yielded to their mutinous crew and seized an opportunity to desert and sail for home. There were now only three ships left to navigate the Strait.

When he saw the ocean, Magellan named it the Pacific, and leaving the strait, stood for the north. For many weeks he sailed with no sight of land. The small stocks of food were quickly used up, and the precious store of fresh water became putrid. Many sailors died of scurvy and privation, and it was then that Magellan proved himself as a leader, steadfast in adversity and a superb navigator. Three months and twenty days passed before an island came in sight.

As the anchors were cast local men ran out to swarm over the ships, stealing anything they could carry away. Magellan replenished his stores with sweet potatoes, figs, bananas, flying fish, coconuts and pigs. He called the islands the Lateen Sail Islands because of the palm leaf sails on the local boats; but the sailors called them the Ladrones, which means 'thieves' in Spanish.

The fleet sailed on through shark infested seas to two outlying islands of the Philippine group

where King Calambu welcomed the officers in his palace, which resembled a thatched barn built up on posts. His admiration for the visitors, their ships and guns, led him to be baptized into the Christian faith. Before Magellan left the islands he became involved in a skirmish with a neighbouring chief on Calambu's behalf, and in the course of it Magellan was killed while covering the retreat of his men.

Thus died one of the finest sailors and navigators of all time. With his primitive instruments he plotted and logged a course that has since been proved to be wonderfully accurate. The local king, embittered by Magellan's defeat, killed the remaining Spanish officers, upon which the crews hurriedly weighed anchor and sailed away.

The *Conception* was burnt, being unserviceable, the remaining two ships sailing to Brunei in Borneo. Here the houses were built upon stilts in the water, the tradeswomen paddling through the town at high tide in boats that were floating shops.

*Mangoes*

For over two years the ships engaged in acts of piracy among the many Pacific Islands, fetching up at last in the Moluccas. Here they found spices, fruits and vegetables, goats and fowls, honey produced by bees the size of ants and parrots of various kinds, the red ones being favourites because they spoke more clearly.

After a long stay the *Victoria* sailed for home, across the Indian Ocean and round the Cape of Good Hope. When the leaky, travel-worn ship reached Spain only eighteen members of the crew were left. People had now to believe the world really was round, and mapmakers were soon busy filling in the great Pacific Ocean, the Philippines, Magellan Strait; and the true size of the earth began to be more accurately judged.

THE SOUTH PACIFIC

Mexico

Philippines

Panama

Borneo

South America

Soloman Islands

Marquesas Isles

Peru

New Hebrides

The Spaniards took full command of the Pacific and its opportunities. Their ships plied between Spanish towns on the west coast of America and the East Indies. In the Philippines the city of Manila was built to be the centre of Spanish authority in the Pacific.

Many Spanish sailors searched eagerly for a great continent that they believed existed in the southern ocean. One of the captains, Sarmiento, discovered the Solomon Islands, and another, Mendaña, came upon the Marquesas. But no continent appeared. Then Quiros, who had been Mendaña's pilot, received a royal command from Spain to make a thorough search of the southern seas. He was given three ships in which provisions, sailors and missionary friars were closely crammed. The ships left Peru in 1605 heavily overladen, their decks cluttered with cattle, pigs, goats and fowls.

Quiros discovered and charted several islands, the chief being the New Hebrides, but the problem of the great new continent remained unsolved.

# THE NORTH PACIFIC

North of Hawaii lies the widest stretch of empty ocean on the globe, and it was in these waters that the Spanish galleons plied between the Philippines and America, linking the ports of Manila, Navidad and Acapulco. The galleons were large and strong, specially built to carry heavy cargoes and many passengers; not easy to manoeuvre and ponderously slow. In the holds was priceless treasure: Chinese silks and embroideries, fine damasks, velvet, linen, carved ivory and sandalwood, jades and jewels. In other holds were spices and herbs from Java, Ceylon and the Moluccas, camphor, musk and borax.

*Sir Francis Drake*

The poorer countries of Europe began to question the right of the Spaniards to a monopoly of all these riches. The English were the first to challenge their power in the audacious attacks on Spanish shipping made by Sir Francis Drake.

*Chinese Jade*

When his ship, the *Golden Hind*, nosed its way out of the Strait of Magellan into the Spanish stronghold, it heralded the slow but sure decline of Spain's supremacy on the seas. Drake was an experienced seaman, a fine navigator and ruthless fighter. Alone he sailed north, under the very bows of the treasure ships, shattering the peace of the Spaniards and spreading alarm throughout the Pacific. When his holds were packed with plunder, Drake deemed it time to return home. He sailed across the Pacific, through the Indies, where he exchanged some of his stolen silver for spices, arriving in England after an absence of three years.

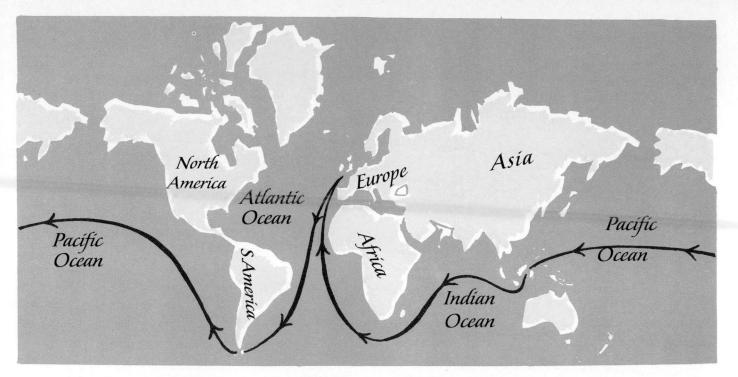

He was the first Englishman to sail round the world in his own flagship, and the first captain to unload in an English port – spices brought direct from the Moluccas.

The Spanish had now to struggle in the Pacific against the attacks of the English and Dutch. They fought on shore and on the sea for power and possession. And while they struggled further north, two Dutch brothers sailed quietly round the foot of South America, giving to the bold headland the name of their ship, the *Horn*, and completing the outline of the map of South America.

# THE SEARCH FOR A NORTHERN PASSAGE

In the northern seas English, French and Dutch sailors were searching for other ways to China and the Spice Islands round the north of America and Asia. Many bays and islands in northern waters bear the names of the sea captains who discovered them while seeking the North-East or North-West Passages: Martin Frobisher, John Davis, William Baffin.

Cartier of France made an important discovery in 1534 when he sailed up the St. Lawrence River and saw the fertile lowlands stretching away on either side. Within fifty years the French were making new homes in Canada. In the east an Englishman had sailed along the coast of Norway to Russia and crossed overland to Moscow. In 1556 Stephen Borough sailed to the Island of Vaigachs where Samoyedes lived in deerskin tents, with deerskin boats which they carried on their backs when on land.

William Barents, a Dutchman, made three voyages in search of a North-East Passage. On the third, in 1596, his ship was crushed in the ice off Novaya Zemlya, an island off the north coast of Russia, and the crew stranded on the mainland for the long arctic winter. They lived in a hut built from driftwood and shot polar bears and foxes for food and clothing. In January they saw the sun for the first time, but could not break through the ice until June. Then they sailed in two open boats through the perilous arctic seas, arriving in Amsterdam in November 1597.

Arctic Circle

Hudson Bay

St. Lawrence River

Another gallant captain was Henry Hudson, who in 1609 sailed to Nova Scotia through the great cod fishing grounds and on up the Hudson River. In Hudson Bay his crew mutinied and set him adrift in a small boat. Hudson was never seen again, but he had added much to our knowledge of the northern seas, and his reports on the abundance of whales greatly encouraged the English whale fishery.

# CAPTAIN JAMES COOK

In the eighteenth century the English and French were still hoping to discover a large continent in the southern oceans, and in 1768 the British Navy sent Captain James Cook into the Pacific, first to make an observation from Tahiti of the transit of the planet Venus across the sun, and then to explore the southern waters.

The *Endeavour*, a sturdy Whitby collier, was fitted out for the voyage in Deptford Yard.

In August she sailed, crossing the Line two months later, and in April reached Tahiti. The transit of Venus was successfully observed in June, and by this time Cook had made friends with the natives. They were cheerful people living on the tropical fruits that grew abundantly all about them; their chief enjoyment, besides wrestling and shooting with bow and arrow, being to sing to the accompaniment of flutes and drums.

Cook left Tahiti for the Antarctic. Doves and albatrosses flew above as he searched vainly in tempestuous seas for a sign of land.

He returned north and sailed completely round the north and south islands of New Zealand, making an excellent chart. He was not the first to discover New Zealand, for Abel Tasman had done that in 1642, though Tasman did not land because of the fierce hostility of the Maoris. These people were angry indeed, but with tact and courage Cook managed to win their confidence.

He sailed westward from New Zealand and sighted Australia. Tasman had previously sailed almost completely round Australia, but had never explored inland. Cook anchored in a good bay and went ashore. The Aboriginals were timid and hid from him, but the surrounding country was full of interesting plants and Cook named the place Botany Bay.

*Australia*

*Tahiti*

*Botany Bay*

*New Zealand*

Later, the *Endeavour* was almost wrecked when she ran on to the Great Barrier Reef, a long wall of rock lying off the north-east coast of Australia. The ship was beached for repairs and Cook took formal possession of the eastern coast of Australia, in the name of George III, calling it New South Wales.

He proceeded to Batavia, by way of Java, and though he had lost no man through scurvy — a great achievement — his crew was now struck down by an epidemic of malaria and dysentery.

By the time the *Endeavour* anchored off Dover in July, 1771, over a third of her crew had died.

On his second voyage, made a year later, Cook was given two ships, the *Resolution* and *Adventure*, and his purpose again was the discovery of land in the south.

But although the ships penetrated far into the Antarctic fogs and icebergs, no land was seen. Cook decided that if a continent did exist it could not possibly be reached because of pack ice, and certainly could not be inhabited. He set course for home, his voyage lasting three years eighteen days.

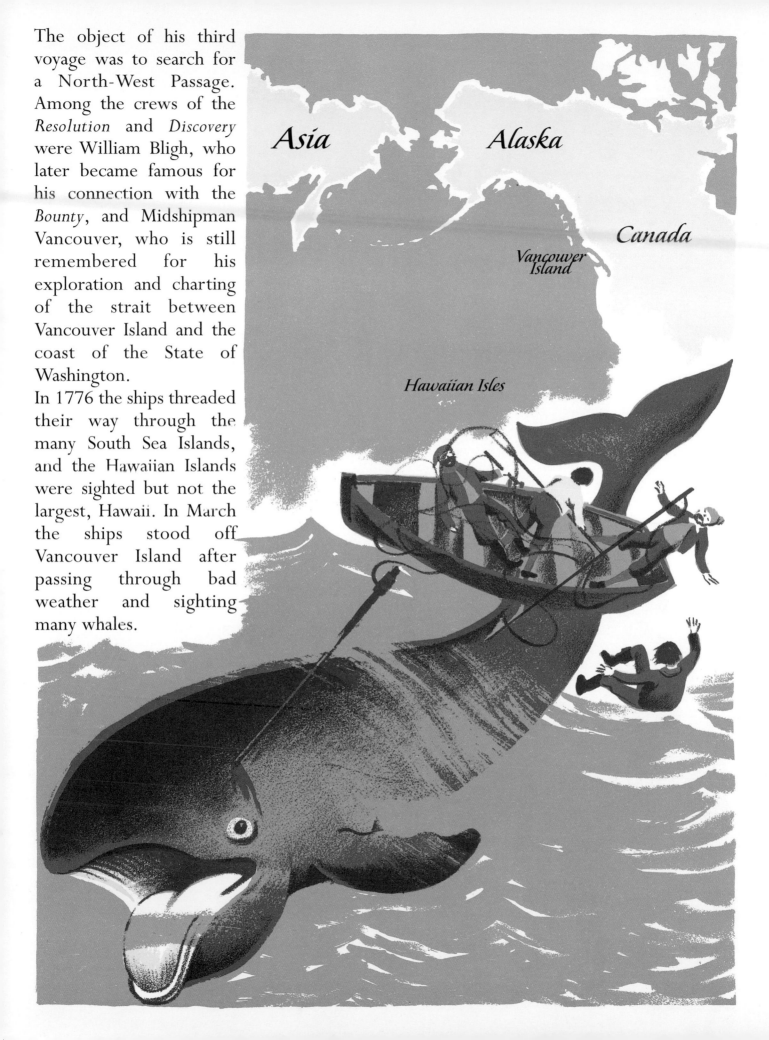

The object of his third voyage was to search for a North-West Passage. Among the crews of the *Resolution* and *Discovery* were William Bligh, who later became famous for his connection with the *Bounty*, and Midshipman Vancouver, who is still remembered for his exploration and charting of the strait between Vancouver Island and the coast of the State of Washington.

In 1776 the ships threaded their way through the many South Sea Islands, and the Hawaiian Islands were sighted but not the largest, Hawaii. In March the ships stood off Vancouver Island after passing through bad weather and sighting many whales.

Asia

Alaska

Canada

Vancouver Island

Hawaiian Isles

Short, plump people came out to trade wolf and bear skins for pieces of brass and iron. They lived in villages, and inside their houses sardines were hung to cure in the smoke of the fires. Behind a hanging mat stood a totem or carved figure, representing a household god, to whom offerings were made.

The ships sailed along the Alaskan coast, investigating every promise of a passage but finding none; through the Aleutian Islands to Bering Strait. Here, on the Asian coast, Cook was met by men dressed all in leather who invited him to their homes.

The search for a passage was continued until Cook was compelled by winter storms and gales to return south.

The island of Hawaii was discovered, and Cook was received with rejoicing being mistaken by the local people for the god of peace. But the

thieving habits of the people proved a source of trouble. When they finally stole the ship's cutter Cook went ashore to protest. His party

was attacked with stones and spears and his men opened fire. Turning to silence the muskets, Cook was clubbed from behind and killed.

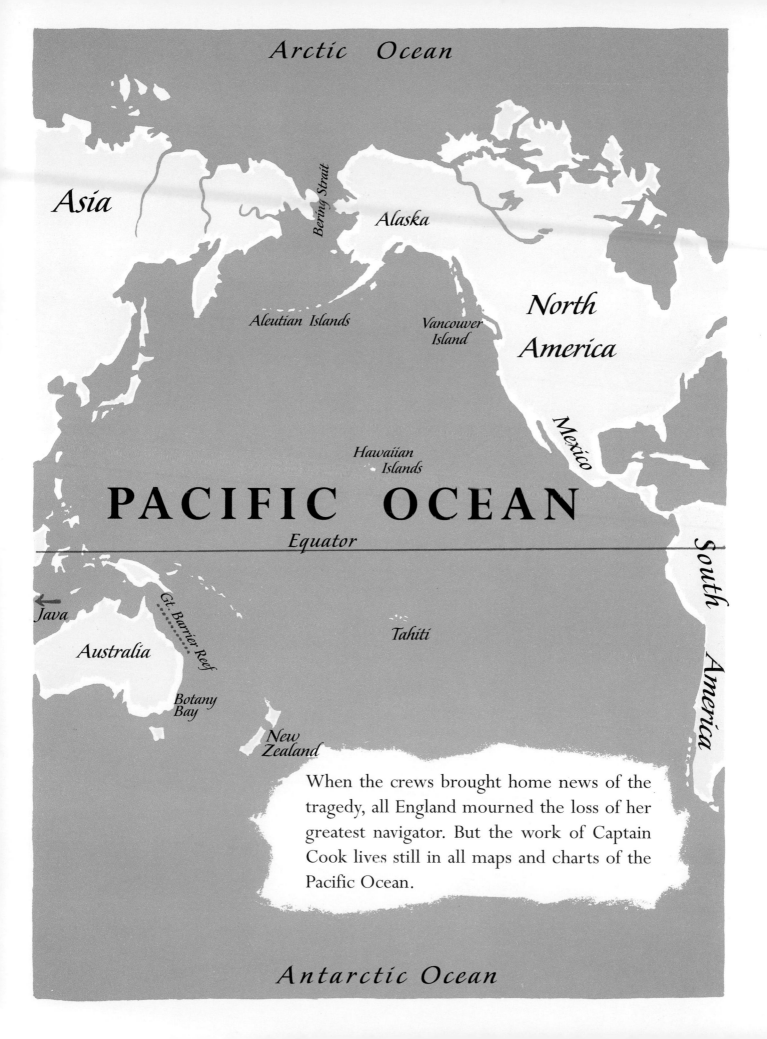

Arctic Ocean

Asia

Bering Strait

Alaska

North
America

Aleutian Islands

Vancouver
Island

Mexico

Hawaiian
Islands

# PACIFIC OCEAN

Equator

South
America

Java

Gt. Barrier Reef

Tahiti

Australia

Botany
Bay

New
Zealand

When the crews brought home news of the tragedy, all England mourned the loss of her greatest navigator. But the work of Captain Cook lives still in all maps and charts of the Pacific Ocean.

Antarctic Ocean

During the seventeenth and eighteenth centuries many fine seamen began to explore the Artic regions more thoroughly.

William Scoresby, an English whaling captain, surveyed the east coast of Greenland.

Sir John Franklin added 1,200 miles to the coastline of North America, exploring the land north of Hudson Bay and westward from the mouth of the Mackenzie River. In 1845 he attempted to master the Northwest Passage from Lancaster Sound to Bering Strait, but the whole expedition perished.

The search parties that went out to find him discovered 7,000 miles of coastline.

By 1847 the outline of the Arctic shores of America was completed.

The Northeast Passage was first mastered by a Swede, Nordenskjold, in 1878.

Fridtjof Nansen, a Norwegian, crossed the great icefield that covers Greenland from east to west in 1887. Later, he tried to reach the North Pole. He believed a strong current ran across the Polar Ocean and that a ship could drift with it, if it were strong enough not to be crushed by the ice. Such a ship was the *Fram* (meaning Forward), a squat, ungainly vessel. She became locked in the ice off the Siberian coast and began slowly to drift northward.

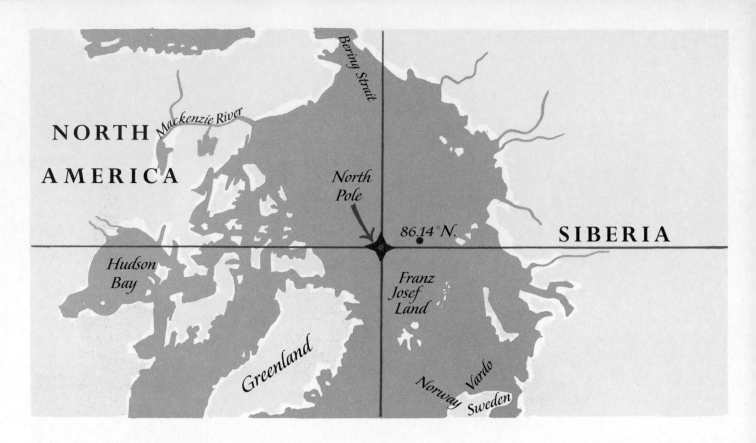

In the first year of drift the *Fram* travelled 189 miles. Then Nansen and a companion tried to reach the Pole overland. They took three sledges, dogs and kayaks, but at 86.14°N. were forced to turn south again. Their journey was difficult and dangerous. They spent the winter in a stone hut on Franz Josef Land, and with the spring set out again on the long trek south.

By chance they walked into the camp of an English explorer waiting for a boat to carry his party home. The Norwegians sailed with them and reached Vardö on August 13, 1896. On the same day the *Fram* broke out of the ice into open sea off Spitzbergen after drifting for thirty-five months.

The first person to reach the North Pole was an American, Robert Peary. He had long experience in Arctic exploration and his expedition was carefully planned. From the observations and soundings he took when he reached the Pole we know that the Central Polar Basin is deep ocean covered with ice that is continually drifting.

North Pole

Another great explorer was Roald Amundsen, born in Norway in 1872, who from the age of fifteen had one purpose in life – to become a polar explorer.

In 1903 he set out to explore the Northwest Passage. His ship was the first to enter Peel Strait, and he dropped anchor in a bay on King William Island. He remained there for two years, and a tribe of Inuit came and built their snow houses round the ship.

They were nomadic hunters of the musk-ox, polar bear, fox and ermine; intelligent, charming and hard-working.

When Amundsen left the harbour, he sailed through a strait where no ship had yet entered. It was shallow and dangerous and progress was slow, but at last a sail was sighted – a whaler out of San Francisco – and Amundsen had reached the open sea. He sailed through Bering Strait and south to San Francisco. He had successfully navigated the Northwest Passage and added much to scientific discovery in the Arctic.

In 1910–1912 Amundsen made his famous expedition to the South Pole. In 1928 he gave his life in an attempt to rescue a friend whose airship had been wrecked in the Arctic.

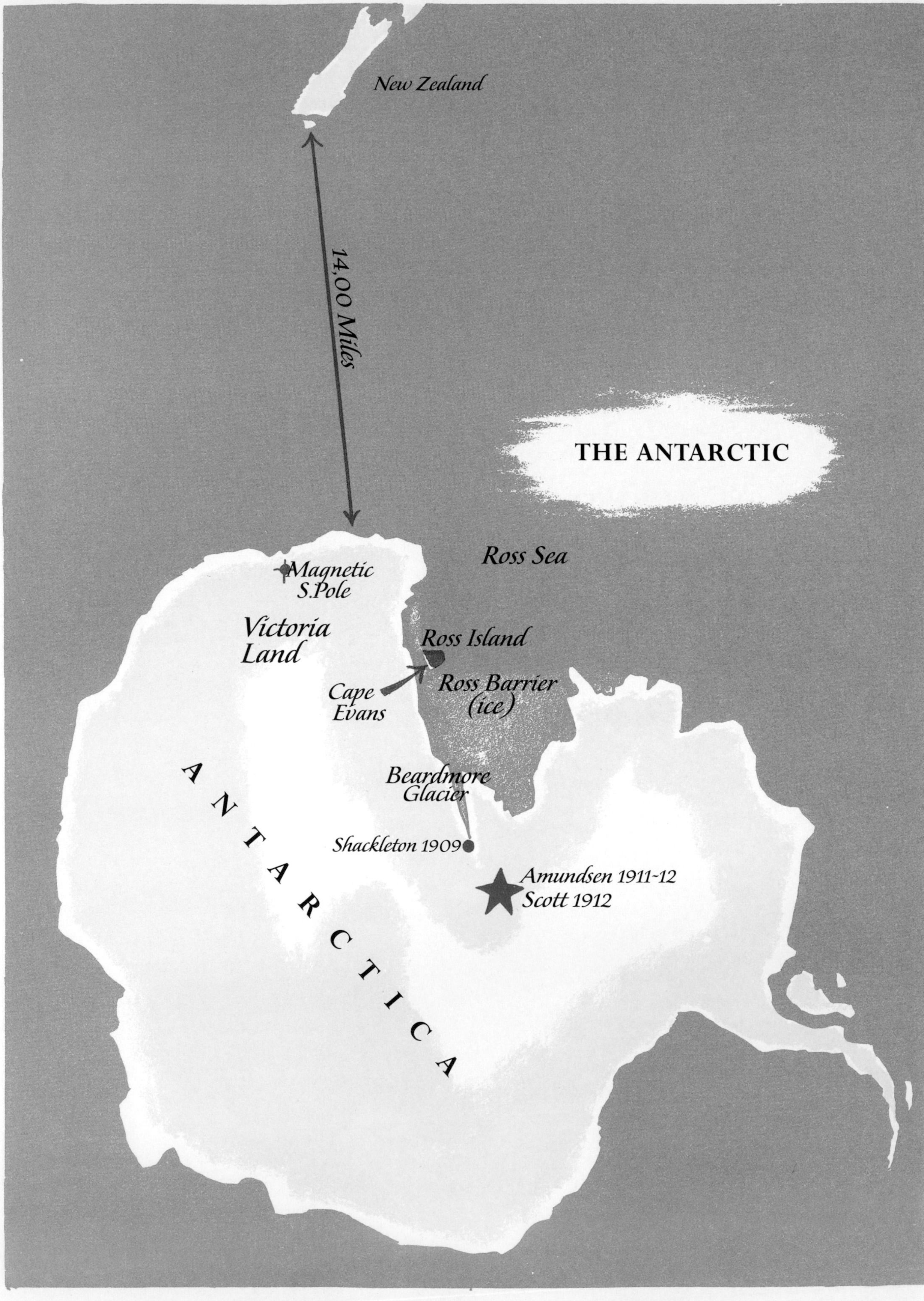

New Zealand

14,00 Miles

THE ANTARCTIC

Ross Sea

Magnetic
S.Pole

Victoria
Land

Ross Island

Cape
Evans

Ross Barrier
(ice)

Beardmore
Glacier

Shackleton 1909

A N T A R C T I C A

Amundsen 1911-12
Scott 1912

The opening up of the Antarctic regions has produced some of the most moving stories of heroism and human endurance ever known in the long history of man.

In 1841 James Ross located the South Magnetic Pole in Victoria Land and came against the 'Barrier', a wall of ice four hundred miles long. The nineteenth century explorers soon realised that there was a large untrodden continent in the Antarctic.

A British Antarctic Expedition was planned and sent out under the command of Robert Falcon Scott.

The chief result of his first expedition was the discovery of the vast plateau that stretches

*Captain Scott*

beyond the Pole. In Scott's party was Sir Ernest Shackleton who, in 1907, made an expedition of his own which reached the South Magnetic Pole and discovered the beautiful and gigantic Beardmore Glacier. Shackleton travelled to within a hundred and eleven miles of the Pole but had to turn back through lack of provisions.

In 1910 Scott set out to discover the South Pole. He left England on June 10. When he reached Melbourne in October a telegram awaited him: "Madeira. Am going south – Amundsen." Thus Scott knew he was in competition with one of the most famous explorers of his day. The British base was at Cape Evans, a distance of 922 miles from the Pole. Motor sledges, ponies and dog teams were to be used, but the motors proved unsuccessful and after three days the men had to continue on foot, pulling a sledge between them. Nor were the ponies happy in the icy conditions, but Captain Oates, by tireless care and kindness, got the best from them.

The marches across the Great Barrier were strenuous and monotonous, a long fight against blizzards and snow-blindness. At the foot of the Beardmore Glacier the ponies were shot, and the men harnessed themselves to the sledges for the long pull to the Pole.

Fossils found in the cliffs of the Glacier included pieces of coal showing tracings of leaves in layers – a sign that tropical forests probably covered the surrounding mountains, millions of years ago. On the Plateau Scott chose Wilson, Oates, P.O. Evans and Bowers to march with him to the Pole. The rest watched until they were a tiny black speck on the horizon. It was the last time anyone saw the five explorers alive.

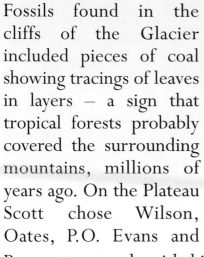

On January 17 the weary men reached the Pole to find the Norwegian flag flying there. Amundsen had beaten them by about 33 days.

On the afternoon of the same day they covered six miles of the return journey. Later they rigged up a sail on the sledge to take advantage of a strong following wind, but had soon to harness themselves again. They were all weakening, and Evans died in harness.

The remaining four pressed on in the vast loneliness. Oates was very ill with frost-bite, and knew he was a drag on the others. On March 16 he walked out of the tent into a blizzard. He walked out to his death so as not to hinder his companions' chance of getting through.

Scott, Wilson and Bowers struggled on to within thirteen miles of their largest depot where food and fuel were stored. But a blizzard forced them to make camp on March 20. They had food for two days and fuel for barely one. They never left that camp, for the blizzard raged on for days, and only their dead bodies and rough notebooks were left to tell a story of unsurpassable courage and endurance.

The problem of the South Pole being solved, French, German and Australasian explorers began to examine in detail the lands and oceans of the Antarctic regions.

One of the most remarkable episodes was Shackleton's expedition in the *Endurance*. He entered the Weddell Sea intending to land and cross the continent to Ross Sea, but it was impossible to put ashore and the *Endurance* drifted north, was crushed in the ice and sank. The men were marooned on an ice floe for nearly six months and finally landed on Elephant Island where their companions were penguins and seals.

Shackleton and five men sailed in an open boat to seek help in South Georgia, and reached the uninhabited side of the island after an epic voyage through ice and storm and tempestuous seas. They crossed the mountains and descended upon the whaling station at Husvik Harbour, nightmare figures with bearded, blackened faces and clothes in rags.

Shackleton's first three attempts to reach Elephant Island failed, but on the fourth he found a passage clear of ice and brought off the stranded men. Since Shackleton's expedition the aeroplane has been used more and more in Antarctic discovery, the most famous flights being made by Admiral R. E. Byrd during the years 1928–1930 and 1933–1935. Gradually the outline of the Continent is taking shape and the character of the country is appearing on the map.

To trace the map of the world in outline, and glimpse the adventures of those who drew it, in terms of courage and vision and hope, is to know only half the story. The other half is told in the exploits of those who filled in the outlines, who explored deep into new lands. Such men as Magellan, Livingstone and Amundsen, beside all the many traders, explorers and pioneers, who between them have made a map not merely a coloured chart but a vivid and enthralling story of adventure and high courage.

Arctic
Ocean

*Greenland*

*Siberia*

*Alaska*

Mackenzie River

Arctic Circle

# Asia

Canada

Hudson
Bay

Vancouver
Island

United States
of America

Nova Scotia

# Atlantic

## Ocean

Bahama
Isles

Hawaii

Mexico

Cuba

Haiti

## Pacific Ocean

Equator

Solomon Isles

Marquesas
Islands

Brazil

New
Hebrides

Tahiti

Australia

South America

The Pope's Line 1494

New
Zealand

Patagonia

Magellan
Strait

East to
Portugal

West to
Spain